HIGH-INTEREST STEAM

MUSIC

HIGH-INTEREST STEAM

AUTOMOBILES
COSMETICS
DRONES
ENVIRONMENT
FASHION
GAMING
MUSIC
SMARTPHONES
SOCIAL MEDIA
SPORTS

HIGH-INTEREST STEAM

MUSIC

STEFANIE ANDURI

MASON CREST
PHILADELPHIA | MIAMI

MASON CREST
PO Box 221876
Hollywood, FL 33022
(866) MCP-BOOK (toll-free) • www.masoncrest.com

First printing

9 8 7 6 5 4 3 2 1
ISBN (hardback) 978-1-4222-4523-1
ISBN (series) 978-1-4222-4516-3
ISBN (ebook) 978-1-4222-7292-3

Library of Congress Cataloging-in-Publication Data

Names: Anduri, Stefanie, author.
Title: Music / Stefanie Anduri.
Description: Hollywood : Mason Crest, 2022. |
Series: High-interest STEAM
Identifiers: LCCN 2019049677 | ISBN 9781422245231 (hardback) |
ISBN 9781422272923 (ebook)
Subjects: LCSH: Music–Acoustics and physics–Juvenile literature. |
Music–Psychological aspects–Juvenile literature. |
Musical instruments–Juvenile literature.
Classification: LCC ML3805 .A534 2022 | DDC 781.1–dc23
LC record available at https://lccn.loc.gov/2019049677

Developed and Produced by National Highlights, Inc.
Editor: Andrew Luke
Production: Crafted Content, LLC

QR CODES AND LINKS TO THIRD-PARTY CONTENT

You may gain access to certain third-party content ("Third-Party Sites") by scanning and using the QR Codes that appear in this publication (the "QR Codes"). We do not operate or control in any respect any information, products, or services on such Third-Party Sites linked to by us via the QR Codes included in this publication, and we assume no responsibility for any materials you may access using the QR Codes. Your use of the QR Codes may be subject to terms, limitations, or restrictions set forth in the applicable terms of use or otherwise established by the owners of the Third-Party Sites. Our linking to such Third-Party Sites via the QR Codes does not imply an endorsement or sponsorship of such Third-Party Sites or the information, products, or services offered on or through the Third-Party Sites, nor does it imply an endorsement or sponsorship of this publication by the owners of such Third-Party Sites.

CONTENTS

KEY ICONS TO LOOK FOR

Words to Understand: These words with their easy-to-understand definitions will increase the readers' understanding of the text while building vocabulary skills.

Sidebars: This boxed material within the main text allows readers to build knowledge, gain insights, explore possibilities, and broaden their perspectives by weaving together additional information to provide realistic and holistic perspectives.

Educational Videos: Readers can view videos by scanning our QR codes, providing them with additional educational content to supplement the text. Examples include news coverage, moments in history, speeches, iconic sports moments, and much more!

Text-Dependent Questions: These questions send the reader back to the text for more careful attention to the evidence presented there.

Research Projects: Readers are pointed toward areas of further inquiry connected to each chapter. Suggestions are provided for projects that encourage deeper research and analysis.

WORDS TO UNDERSTAND

cymatics—the study of waves (i.e. sound waves) and their impact on the world around them. Pioneered by Swiss natural scientist Hans Jenny, it is derived from the Greek words "kyma" meaning wave and "ta kymatica" meaning matters pertaining to waves

psychoacoustics—a branch of science dealing with the perception of sound, the sensations produced by sounds, and the problems of communication

synesthesia—a subjective sensation or image of a sense (as of color) other than the one (as of sound) being stimulated

CHAPTER 1

SCIENCE IN MUSIC

Science and music may seem like very different fields of study, but the two have all kinds of amazing connections. From the ways instruments and voices produce sound, to the ways that sound vibrations affect our bodies and the world around us, the links between science and music are mind-blowing. Without music, life on earth would be very different.

HOW INSTRUMENTS MAKE SOUND

Sound is created by vibration. Whenever a musician plays an instrument, it creates a sound wave that wiggles the air molecules around it. The sound waves create wiggly air molecules that move through space until they reach a listener's ears. Then the sound waves travel through the listener's ears, causing the structures of the ear to vibrate. The listener's brain perceives these vibrations as sound.

Musical instruments create vibration in various ways. There are four main categories of musical instruments: winds, brass,

Wind instruments like clarinets work by blowing air past a reed, causing it to vibrate.

percussion, and strings. Winds (such as clarinets, flutes, saxophones, oboes, recorders, and bassoons) and brass instruments (such as trumpets, trombones, tubas, and horns) create sound waves when the player creates vibrations at the instrument's mouthpiece either by buzzing their lips together, by blowing air past a reed that vibrates, or by blowing air through an opening in the instrument that creates a whistling effect. Then the air moves through the bodies of the instruments and echoes to create resonance, which makes the original vibrations louder. String instruments (violins, violas, cellos, upright basses, guitars, and harps) create sound when the strings are either plucked or bowed, causing them to vibrate, and the hollow body of the instrument resonates the sound. Some percussion instruments, such as drums, xylophone, glockenspiel, bells, timpani, and cymbals vibrate when they are struck, and here the instrument, itself, vibrates. Other percussion instruments, such as maracas, must be shaken to create vibration. Keyboard instruments fall into multiple categories. Pianos are a combination of percussion and strings. When a pianist plays a note, it causes an internal hammer to strike a string, which creates sound. Pipe organs, on the other hand, are more like wind instruments. They create sound when keys are pressed down, sending air through the corresponding pipes. The human voice is like wind instruments; the voice needs air to work. After the lungs fill up with air, the body releases that air through the vocal folds, which vibrate to create sound. The air then moves through the throat (pharynx) and out of the mouth. The pharynx also helps the sound waves to resonate and become louder.

String instruments like violins create sound by using something, like a bow, pick, or fingers, to pluck the strings and cause them to vibrate.

In brass and wind instruments, the scientific principle known as the Bernoulli effect is on display.

In brass and wind instruments and in human voices, air is one of the most basic factors. Science has helped us figure out just how these instruments work. Most people have heard that the Bernoulli effect helps airplanes fly, but it is less common knowledge that the Bernoulli effect is also important in music. This scientific principle teaches that fast moving air creates lower pressure, which creates suction. That fast-moving air is necessary to keep instruments playing and voices singing through phrases. When lips, vocal folds, or reeds are squeezed together and air is forced through, the Bernoulli effect pushes them apart and sucks them back together hundreds, or even thousands, of times per second. This is called vibration. The faster the vibration, the higher the pitch.

PSYCHOACOUSTICS

Music is everywhere. Sometimes we don't even realize how often music is playing in the background. From stores to restaurants to movies, the music we hear, both consciously and subconsciously, sends a message to our bodies. For example, a strong, fast beat can speed up a person's heart rate, breath, or brain waves. It can make toes tap or heads bop almost involuntarily. By contrast, a slower music with a softer beat can make our heart rates slow down. Some research suggests that listening to music composed during the Baroque era (1600–1750 AD) while studying can help the brain absorb material more quickly and thoroughly. The body's reaction to music is measured in a type of science called **psychoacoustics**. This field of study is both fascinating and useful. It can help business owners, marketers, film score composers, DJs, or commercial directors to make their endeavors more effective. Utilizing the concept of psychoacoustics, some restaurants play fast music in order to encourage diners to eat quickly. This then ensures that more clients are served, as tables open up more quickly. And some stores play slow, gentle music to make their clients feel comfortable. In fact, there are companies that use psychoacoustics to create custom-made playlists for their clients. There are even companies who specialize in creating playlists to calm down pets who get nervous when their families are away. Music has a huge, measurable impact on our bodies and, especially, our brains.

Music also evokes memories and the emotions associated with them. That's why holiday music can make a person feel immediately excited, or hearing a familiar lullaby can bring back a memory from childhood. But it can also help cement new memories.

At certain restaurants, fast-paced music is played as a tactic to get diners to eat more quickly.

MOOD MUSIC

The music we choose to listen to says a lot about who we are and how we are feeling in the moment. Fast music with a strong beat can get blood pumping before a sporting event. A sweet lullaby can lull a baby to sleep. A sad song can bring us solace after a breakup. Music can bring out romantic feelings or provide an outlet for anger. It can soothe anxiety. Music is an incredibly powerful tool for experiencing and shaping human emotions.

This information can be helpful for test preparation. Because music and memory are linked, creating a song using words, facts, or equations can make studying both easier and more fun.

Because of music's impact on the brain and body, movie score composers use psychoacoustics to give subtle background clues. In the movie *Jaws*, everyone feels the suspense that builds when the musical theme begins to play in the background. As the music speeds up, so does the listener's heart rate. In a similar fashion, a romantic comedy wouldn't feel so romantic if the music in the background of every kissing scene sounded like it belonged in a horror movie. Instead, it might signal some impending doom. And how strange would it seem for circus music to play in the background of a tragic movie scene? In movie scores, the music is intended to intensify the emotions and to convey information that the movie, itself, could not. It is meant to evoke a strong emotional response to the movie so that audiences are encouraged to watch it again and again.

Music is a central part of religious and spiritual practices worldwide.

Music is also a central part of most religions and spiritual practices throughout the world. Various forms of chant exist in Jewish, Orthodox Christian, Catholic, Hindu, Buddhist, and Muslim religious ceremonies, among others. Hymnal and worship music is common in much of the Protestant world. Indigenous tribes around the world use music in spiritual celebrations. Music can deepen bonds between people, it can ingrain emotional memories into our minds, and it can bring about a state of calm that aids in prayer and meditation. No wonder it is such a common element of spiritual practice!

MUSIC THERAPY

Like psychoacoustics, music therapy explores how music affects the brain and body. But unlike psychoacoustics, music therapy focuses on the medical effects of music on humans. Music has been found to alleviate symptoms of many health issues including Parkinson's disease, Alzheimer's, Autism spectrum disorders, learning disabilities, mood and mental health disorders, and sleep disorders, among many others. It can aid in drug and injury rehabilitation. There is even evidence that playing music to a pregnant woman's belly can cause her baby to develop more healthfully.

Music activates the whole brain. Because of this incredible ability, music therapists use it as a tool to heal the brain and help it to create new synaptic connections. Music therapy can encourage the brain to learn and focus differently, it can help the brain create a sense of order, it can cause the brain to release a feel-good chemical called dopamine, it can offer listeners an emotional outlet that

Studies have shown that playing music for a baby in utero helps with healthy development.

reduces stress, and it can improve speech and communication in people with brain injuries or speech difficulties. Music is a powerful medicine.

CYMATICS

In order to understand the incredible world of **cymatics**, it's important to know a few mind-blowing facts about sound and vibration.

1. Everything that vibrates makes sound, and everything that makes sound vibrates. Sound and vibration go hand-in-hand.
2. At the tiniest level, all matter in the universe vibrates. Even when something looks like it is a solid and motionless object, it is vibrating like crazy at the atomic level.

Like ocean waves, sound waves also have distinct and unique patterns.

Technologist Evan Grant shares cymatic experiments and explores why the field of cymatics is useful in our world.

That means that every single object in the universe is always making noise. Imagine how noisy it would be if your ears could hear all that sound. Luckily, human ears are only able to perceive a small range of the noises that exist around us at all times. The other senses pick up vibrations at frequencies that the ears do not perceive. So in a way, eyes "hear" light, noses "hear" smells, and tongues "hear" tastes.

When ocean waves roll back and forth across the beach sand, they leave a pattern behind. Sound waves aren't so different. Unlike water waves, sound waves can't be seen, but the patterns they leave behind are visible. The study of cymatics examines the impact that sound waves have on the world around us. Scientists first observed the effect of sound waves on shapes and forms as early as the 1500s. Leonardo da Vinci and Galileo Galilei both observed the

WEIRD MUSICAL SCIENCE

In addition to all the fascinating ways music shapes our minds, our bodies, and our world, it does some pretty strange things too. For example, imagine how bizarre it would be to attend a concert of your favorite band and realize the music is visible. For people with **synesthesia**, this phenomenon can be real. Synesthetes get their sensation wires crossed. This means that something most people perceive with only one sense—such as *hearing* music—is perceived by the expected sense plus at least one more—like *seeing* or *tasting* music. Music might evoke images of colors, shapes, or textures. It might bring about a memorable scent or taste. It could even *feel* a certain way. Synesthesia doesn't only affect how people perceive sound. For some synesthetes, a color can taste a certain way or a number can evoke a smell. What an interesting way to experience the world!

effect of sound waves on a metal plate covered in grains of sand. They vibrated the metal plate with a violin bow and saw that the sand created certain patterns when vibrated at different pitches. In modern cymatic experiments, scientists put a plate of liquid (like water) or powder (like sand) on top of a speaker. When different sounds play through the speaker, the liquid or powder reacts by forming incredible patterns. The patterns formed look just like other patterns in nature, such as those seen in snowflakes, oils, water, salts, flower petals, seeds, and animal scales, among many other things. The field of cymatics has revealed that sound waves were crucial to the formation of our universe. Though it isn't always

The phenomenon of having a song "stuck in your head" is one scientists cannot explain, but its universality is a testament to the power of music.

possible to hear (at least with our ears) all the sounds around us, we know they have a big impact on shaping our world and our universe.

Everyone knows how annoying it can be to get a tune stuck in his or her head. Sometimes these so-called "earworms" get stuck on repeat for days. Scientists aren't quite sure what exactly causes this phenomenon, but they do believe it has something to do with the simplicity and repetitiveness of the tune and the emotional connection we have to it. Maybe someday, there will be a cure, but until then, music is contagious.

Even more bizarre than earworms are musical hallucinations. People who experience musical hallucinations actually *hear* the music with their ears. This is different from earworms, which exist just in thoughts. Brain injuries, seizures, drugs or drug withdrawal, or psychiatric conditions can bring these on.

The connections between music and science are amazing. Music helps to shape cultures, minds, and bodies, and even the world. It is an innate part of human experiences. It is impossible to know all the ways in which the link between science and music affects the world, but it is fascinating to dig deeper into this incredible connection to find just how music helps form our lives.

TEXT-DEPENDENT QUESTIONS

1. What do people study in the field of psychoacoustics?
2. How are cymatic patterns created?
3. How does an instrument create sound?

RESEARCH PROJECT

Listen to the below-listed pieces of music and take note of how your body responds. Calculate your heart and breath rates for each and draw conclusions about how each piece affects your body.

1. *Music for 18 Musicians* by Steve Reich
2. *Such Great Heights* by Iron and Wine
3. *Blackwater Park* by Opeth
4. *Ipofero* by Despina Vandi
5. *Threnody for the Victims of Hiroshima* by Krzysztof Penderecki

WORDS TO UNDERSTAND

amplification—an act, example, or product of increasing the strength or amount of something

Auto-Tune—the brand name of the technology that improves pitch accuracy in live or recorded music

theremin—a musical instrument with electronic tone generation, the pitch and tone volume being controlled by the distance between the player's hands and two metal rods serving as antennas

CHAPTER 2

TECHNOLOGY IN MUSIC

Technology has an enormous impact on the way we experience music. Without technology, the only way to hear music would be in a live performance. But even *that* wouldn't be the same. It's obvious that technology influences how we listen to music, but it also influences how music sounds, how instruments are made, how musicians train themselves to play their instruments, and the scientific understanding of how music functions and how it impacts the world around us.

LISTENING TECHNOLOGY

Whether you're listening to the car radio, an MP3 player, or Spotify, technology is crucial to music in the modern world. If music technology didn't exist, it would be nearly impossible to listen to new artists. We could only hear our favorite bands when they played in our hometowns. Music composed before our lifetime would be rarely performed. It would be impossible to listen to famed voices of the past like Louis Armstrong, Etta James, Elvis Presley, John

Technology has made it possible to listen to an almost limitless amount of music practically anywhere.

Lennon, Roger Waters, or Whitney Houston. There would be no music videos, no SOUNDCLOUD, no Pandora. There would be no film or video game scores because movies and video games would not exist. And since each generation of musicians is influenced by the generations before it, music, itself, would have evolved differently. World music would be influenced almost entirely by culture, rather than by other musicians. Technology has globalized music in interesting ways. Before the technological age, music varied more from region to region. For example, Italian music could be easily distinguished from German and French music. Today, it is sometimes difficult to distinguish American music from music of any other region. And though this intermixing of styles may blur cultural lines, it allows musicians to be inspired by one another to create more art.

RECORDING TECHNOLOGY

It actually wouldn't even matter that *listening* technology didn't exist, because without technology, artists would have no way of recording their music in the first place. Recording technology can be as simple as a big red button on an iPhone screen or as complex as an intricate soundboard at a recording studio. It can balance a sound to make sure all the instruments are heard. It can make a sound warmer and gentler or brassier and more aggressive by choosing which elements to highlight. It can speed a song up or slow it down. Recording technology can incorporate extra sounds like sirens, animal noises, clips from other songs, and so on. It can distort music or add reverberation. It can loop a specific section of a song or allow an artist to harmonize with himself/herself. That's how musicians like Imogen Heap can sing entire chords by themselves.

Sound technology is essential to the live performance of music.

Guitar strings and drumsticks can be easily replaced. The same is not true for a singer's voice, which may require occasional rest.

MUSIC TECHNOLOGY IN LIVE MUSIC SETTINGS

In live performances, sound technology is essential. Sound technicians at concerts have to be in tune with all of the instruments on the stage. When a certain instrument has a solo, the sound technician makes sure it can be heard. When the audience gets loud, the sound technician might respond by adding extra volume. Sound technicians can dub in sound effects, background tracks, or even all the vocals for an entire concert. More than one performing artist has been caught lip-synching at a concert in the past—stars like Whitney Houston, Mariah Carey, and Brittney Spears have been caught red-handed. Although a paying audience might feel disgruntled to learn that their favorite performer isn't actually *singing* the concert, this technology can be extremely helpful in certain situations. When a guitar breaks a string or a drummer splits a drumstick, it can be easily and quickly replaced. However, when a singer is ill or his or her voice is exhausted, it is more difficult to replace. Especially on long concert tours, voices need rest. It might be a bummer to miss out on the real live thing, but having the ability to dub in the vocals means that a show can go on, rather than being canceled altogether.

In musical theatre productions, balancing numerous headset microphones can be a grueling task. When multiple voices are meant to blend, a sound technician is responsible for making sure that the people with powerful voices don't overshadow the people with lighter voices. This balance may change throughout a performance, as different parts of each singer's voice might produce more or less sound. Sound technicians have to be aware of the orchestra too. Sometimes the orchestral music swells when a singer is in a part of his or her range where they need extra amplification. Sometimes

Sound technicians must balance the highs and lows of musical performances, with the notable exception of operas, where singers do not use amplification.

a singer's voice suddenly explodes on a high note. The sound technician is responsible for making the sound both comfortable and emotionally enthralling for the audience. If the sound is too loud and heavy throughout a performance, it becomes overstimulating. If the sound is too soft throughout without any variation, it lacks excitement. It is when the musical and dramatic peaks and valleys of a show are well balanced that audiences have an amazing experience.

AUTO-TUNE

Auto-Tune is another piece of technology that has a major impact on the way music sounds. As its name suggests, Auto-Tune is useful for tuning voices that are not always on pitch. Sometimes, especially in live concerts with rowdy audiences, a singer can have a hard time hearing which notes to sing. A lot of athletic motion can also cause pitch to struggle, since being out-of-breath can make singing—especially high notes—difficult. And often a singer's pitch can be affected by nervousness. Auto-Tune bends the pitch so that it sounds precisely like where it ought to be. It also creates a mechanical or robotic sound that is popular in many different musical styles. Auto-Tune is commonly used in both live performances and recordings.

AMPLIFICATION

Music wouldn't be music as we know it without **amplification**. Microphones and electric instruments such as guitars and keyboards need to be plugged into amplifiers, which are then plugged into speakers. Amplification allows musicians (and especially singers) to use their instruments more healthfully. Amplification also allows for sound effects such as distortion, reverberation, and delay. It can

Music technology students and faculty at the Massachusetts Institute of Technology discuss the importance of music technology education.

bring out certain tone qualities and diminish others. If there were no amplifiers, radios would not have worked. Without amplification, artists could only perform for hundreds of people rather than thousands, or even millions if the performance is being broadcast. Modern music would certainly be sparse without technology.

There are different types of microphones for different jobs. A sound technician has to know which mic is right for each performance. Some microphones work best for acoustic instruments, some are intended for voices, while others function best with heavy sounds, like a drum kit. Sometimes mics are attached to a stand, sometimes they hang from the ceiling in front of the performers, and sometimes they are attached to a performer's face or chest. Microphones are versatile because performances vary so drastically. Some performers, such as public speakers, may stand

Electric amplifiers have been around in one form or another since the 1930s.

mostly still. Some, such as pop stars, may incorporate lots of athletic dancing that would make a hand-held mic impossible. In live theatre performances, mics are more likely to be hanging just above the performers' heads or attached via headset.

EVOLUTION OF LISTENING

Music-listening technology has evolved substantially since it was created in the 1870s. The first form of recording technology was the phonograph, which was created by Thomas Edison. It was capable of both recording and playing back sound. Over time, the phonograph's sound quality improved drastically. In the 1940s, cassette tapes took over as the most popular type of recording technology. Cassette tapes were preferred because they could hold more music and their sound was clearer. In the 1980s, CDs became the favored form of music technology. However, CDs proved to be quite delicate, so after just a few years in the limelight, MP3s rocketed into first place. At the same time, phonographs and vinyl records made a huge comeback in popular culture. Enthusiasts believe records have better sound quality than other forms of music technology. In recent years, streaming apps and websites and digital music storage sites like iTunes have taken over. What will they think of next?

ELECTRONIC MUSIC

It would be impossible to talk about music technology without mentioning electronic music. Today, Electronic Dance Music (EDM) is the type of electronic music that comes to mind, but throughout the technological age, there have been many applications of electronics

Thomas Edison invented the phonograph in 1877.

in music. In the 20th century, classical composers started to take huge risks like never before. Composers like Philip Glass, Steve Reich, Milton Babbitt, Edgar Varèse, and Terry Reiley used technology in new and exciting ways in their music. In the 1920s, a new electronic instrument called the **theremin** was created. This unique instrument is played without being touched. The distance between the musician's hands and the instrument determines pitches. A theremin's sound is easy to identify because it always sounds spooky. In old movies, it was sometimes used to imitate a ghost. Today, pop music of all genres is full of electronic music. Whenever a DJ mixes a new track, or a rap artist samples someone else's song and incorporates it into his or her own, it's all electronic music.

DJs use a wide variety of technology to remix music while spinning at clubs.

EDM

Electronic Dance Music (EDM) is the purest form of electronic music because it doesn't usually include any live musicians. EDM artists either create mixes from a huge combination of pre-recorded sounds, or they produce their own. Artists like Daft Punk, Tiësto, and Deadmau5 have gained international recognition and popularity for their music. Although EDM was originally created for clubs and raves, it has become mainstream in recent years. It's nearly impossible to turn on the radio without hearing the most recent EDM hits.

ACOUSTIC ANALYSIS

In order to analyze how music and sound work, scientists developed forms of technology that measure various elements of sound. Our ears perceive the noises we hear as simple sounds. But under the surface, sound is a complex and complicated thing to understand. Looking more deeply, sound is layered with overtones—extra frequencies that add different flavors to the sound. Overtones might make a sound brighter or darker, softer or louder, warmer or brassier. Acoustic analysis software helps detect all the details of the sounds around us.

Spectral analysis technology has been around since the 1940s. Now, it's so common and simple that there are cell phone apps that analyze sounds picked up by the device's microphone. Spectral analysis is a phenomenal tool for aspiring musicians because it can give precise information about the sounds being produced. This type of software is especially common among opera singers in-training who hope to teach their bodies how to produce unamplified sounds over an orchestra in a large hall. It is beneficial for these musicians to understand the correlation between how they sing and the quality of the sounds produced.

Technology has also been developed to measure the impact of music on human brains and bodies. Biofeedback technology measures music's impact on body functions such as heart rate, breath rate, and brain waves. This technology is beneficial to psychoacoustics researchers and music therapists who use its information to make music beneficial to more people.

Biofeedback technology is just one of many technologies that has been developed to measure the impact of music on the human brain.

MOVIE MUSIC

Many forms of technology depend on music to tell a story. A music soundtrack is a critical part of video games, commercials, television, and movies. Background music enhances the plots of these forms of entertainment because it provides clues to the silent emotions or motives of the characters or their situations. Without music, these types of media would be less compelling.

EXTRA-MUSICAL USES OF TECHNOLOGY

Technology's impact on music goes beyond its ability to enhance or reproduce sound. In many musical performances, visual effects are nearly as important as sound. Lighting, projections, and subtitles or supertitles are necessary components of many shows. A spotlight can help an audience and a videographer follow the lead performer around a dark stage. Other lighting effects can add drama, color, and excitement to a stage. Pyrotechnics can make a performance feel explosive and thrilling. Sometimes, especially in performances sung in foreign languages, there are subtitles or supertitles to assist the audience in understanding what the performers are saying. In fact, some large opera houses such as the Metropolitan Opera in New York City have small screens attached to every chair. These screens offer to translate each performance into a number of languages to accommodate audience members from around the world.

Advertising for musical events would be limited without technology. The most common forms of advertising include radio announcements, Internet and music streaming app ads, social media posts, and television commercials. Without technology, none of these types of marketing could exist. If music were so difficult to gain access to, it would be difficult to incorporate it into society.

Music existed before the advent of technology, but the advent of music technology has drastically improved music's accessibility. It makes listening to recordings possible. It allows us to connect to musicians of the past, it improves sound quality and balance, it gives music variety, it incorporates music into movie and video game plots, and it provides professional musicians with new ways to train themselves to better use their instruments. Without music technology, beloved music of all genres and eras would be lost. It's impossible to know just what music would sound like if music technology didn't exist, but we can be certain that it wouldn't be the same.

With the advent of technology, music is more accessible than ever before.

TEXT-DEPENDENT QUESTIONS

1. What does an amplifier do?
2. What are some ways in which computers are helpful to musicians?
3. What is Auto-Tune?

RESEARCH PROJECT

At a local music store, ask to test various types of microphones. Record the differences you hear through each of the mics.

Next, gradually adjust each of the different knobs on the amplifier, recording the results as you go.

Research the way each microphone functions; infer the reasons they all create different sounds. Research how the amplifier works, and how each of the knobs alters the sound.

WORDS TO UNDERSTAND

acoustics—the qualities or characteristics of a room, auditorium, stadium, etc., that determine the audibility or fidelity of sounds in it

lyre—a musical instrument of ancient Greece consisting of a sound box made typically from a turtle shell, with two curved arms connected by a yoke from which strings are stretched to the body, used especially to accompany singing and recitation

soundboard—an electronic board used to mix acoustic information

CHAPTER 3

ENGINEERING IN MUSIC

Engineering has played a crucial role in the development of new technologies and instruments that have ushered in new styles of music for thousands of years. Engineering is all about using the known laws of physics to create new things. In the music world, engineering is used to create new and better instruments, recording technology, amplification technology, and **acoustic** spaces, all of which provide us with better sound quality and new types of music to play and hear.

EVOLUTION OF MUSIC INSTRUMENT CONSTRUCTION AND DESIGN

Music has been a part of humanity since pre-historic times. Historians believe ancient cultures around the world created percussion by hitting sticks or rocks together or by using some form of baton on hollow objects such as logs. Archeologists have unearthed flutes dating back over 40,000 years (some archeologists estimate the earliest instruments discovered date back as far as

60,000 years). Ancient instruments were handmade from whatever materials were available. Flutes were often carved out of animal bones. It is thought that early drums were made out of animal skins, but because skins disintegrate, there is little proof for this theory. For much of ancient history, music making was limited to these instruments and, of course, the human voice.

The first string instruments are thought to have been created roughly around 3,000 BCE in what is now Egypt and the Middle East. They typically consisted of harps and **lyres**. Wall paintings from ancient Egyptian civilizations show harps made from hunters' bows. Lyres were made of wood, as were their bows. The strings of these instruments were typically made of animal guts. Various forms of string instruments dating back nearly as far as those found in Egypt have been discovered around the world. Some had only two strings, while

This statue in Paris, France, is of a woman holding a lyre, one of the world's oldest stringed instruments.

DIDGERIDOOS

Roughly 10,000 years ago, Aboriginal people of Australia made the first didgeridoo. Actually, that's not entirely true. Termites were the ones that created the first wind instruments. These insects munched on eucalyptus trees enough to hollow out their branches. Aboriginal people noticed that the wind made a lovely whistling sound as it passed through the eucalyptus trees and from there they learned how to reproduce that sound. Though it is used around the world today, the didgeridoo is still primarily associated with the Aboriginal culture of Australia.

some had many more. Some had bows and some did not. All of these instruments did have two things in common: they had strings that could vibrate and their bodies could serve as mini echo chambers.

The family of instruments we now call "brass instruments" is comprised of trumpets, trombones, tubas, euphoniums, and several other instruments. The earliest instruments in this family date back to 1500 BCE. They were simple, straight horns made mostly of silver and bronze. There were even horn instruments discovered in King Tut's grave! Early horns did not have buttons, so to change pitches, the musicians had to adjust the way they used their breath and their buzzing lips. These instruments were only capable of playing a few pitches.

Over time, as tools and machinery improved and musical demands changed, so did instruments. Brass instruments gradually developed better sound quality and became easier to play. Stringed instruments evolved over the centuries to meet the needs of the music of their time. Today, the most desired string instruments

Woodwind instruments produce a wide range of timbres and pitches.

are precisely carved out of specific types of wood. The materials are carefully chosen and crafted because the body has a huge responsibility: it amplifies its sound. It also has a big impact on the instrument's sound quality. Modern strings are made of nylon or steel rather than animal guts. Their bows are made of wood and horsehair. Percussion instruments, which began as sticks, logs, and rocks, are now numerous and varied. Drums are the best-known percussion instruments, but this family of instruments also includes tympani, cymbals, marimbas, xylophones, and many others. Some percussion instruments are unique to specific cultures.

Woodwind instruments have evolved with more capabilities. Unlike the earliest flutes, modern woodwinds are not typically made of bone. The materials used to make them vary since the instruments in this family range from saxophones to clarinets, oboes, and bassoons. Unlike brass instruments, which require the musicians to buzz their lips to produce any sound, woodwinds produce sound when air either passes through a reed or is blown over the edge of the mouthpiece of the instrument. The variety of instruments in this category allows for a wide range of timbres (tone colors) and pitch ranges.

The evolution of instruments was a result of growing musical demands. As music became more technically difficult and performing spaces got much bigger, instruments had to be created to accommodate these demands. According to the evidence available, when early instruments were created, they were only used to play simple music, which often accompanied a voice. Throughout music history, music has changed drastically. The earliest forms of western music involved unison voices with very little instrumentation. It evolved to include symphonies, operas, chamber music, and solo music. Some music moves quickly, while some moves slowly. Some stays within a moderate range, while some requires the extremes of an instrument's range. When concert halls got larger and the first orchestras formed, instruments had to grow along with them. They had to be able to be heard far from the stage, all the way in the back of a performance venue. As music continues to change, so will the need for new instruments. This is why courses like Yale University's *Musical Acoustics and Instrument Design* exist. Students enrolled in this course learn the engineering behind how sound and music function, and then design, build, and play their new instrument in class.

SOUND ENGINEERING

Sound engineers have a crucial job. They are responsible for the balance and clarity of sound in performance spaces and recording studios. They record performances and adjust microphone levels. They incorporate special sound effects. They are responsible for the clarity of the sound. After a track is recorded, sound engineers are responsible

Sound engineers are responsible for the balance and clarity of sound for live performances and studio recordings.

for mixing and editing each track before it is released. Without sound engineers, the music we listen to would sound much less polished.

Sound engineers are also responsible for mixing the sound in live performances so that audiences get the clearest and most balanced sound possible. This is an absolute necessity for any commercial music concerts, such as rock, pop, hip-hop, etc., but sound engineers can also be employed in classical music. In fact, there are some pieces of music that include very specific instructions for sound engineers. In 1964, a man named Milton Babbitt wrote a piece called *Philomel.* Performances of it use both live and electronic components. In this bizarre, eerie, and intriguing piece, four or more speakers are placed around the concert hall. The live soprano is involved in a sort of conversation with the voice coming from the speakers, which is actually a synthetic version of her own voice. In performances, the audience is surrounded by sound. It's like being caught in the middle of a conversation between two friends. Sound engineers are responsible for creating this effect.

COMPUTER ENGINEERING

Computer software engineers are a bigger part of the music industry today than ever in the past. New games, applications, and websites are being created all the time. Much of the world has integrated this technology into their daily lives. Apps like *iHeartRADIO, Pandora, Spotify,* and *YouTube,* as well as educational music programs like *Finale, Sibelius,* and *GarageBand* were all created by computer software engineers. Software engineers helped create games like *Guitar Hero* and *Rock Band*.

Sound analysis technologies are increasingly common tools in music schools throughout the country. Programs such as *VoceVista* are used for sound analysis. As a musician sings or plays music, they provide feedback in the form of a spectrograph. This can be an effective tool in teaching musicians how to improve the way they play.

Music streaming platform Spotify is a popular example of several computer applications that have been developed by computer engineers.

Software engineers work with developers to create video games, which have extensively integrated music as part of the gaming experience.

In 2009, a musical phenomenon occurred. A young woman recorded herself singing a famous piece of choral music, and viewers responded by adding their own recordings of the same piece. A virtual choir was formed! Today, virtual choirs and orchestras are more and more common. Computer engineers are the catalyst for global musical connection. In 2013, renowned composer Eric Whitacre included a live performance of a virtual choir in a TED talk. He included a large in-person choir in the performance as well. Virtual ensembles provide an incredible opportunity to create art with people from around the world. They offer people from opposing beliefs or dueling countries a unique chance to create beauty together. It is a phenomenal way to link music and computer engineering.

ELECTRICAL ENGINEERING

Without electrical engineers, there would be no microphones, amps, speakers, or headphones. There would be no **soundboards**

At Eastman School of Music (Rochester, NY), students and faculty work together to improve music technology.

or lighting effects. There would be no radios, computers, phones, or other listening devices. Every time a rock star plays an iconic electric guitar solo, they depend on the use of an amplifier to be heard in the audience. Every time a famous singer presents the National Anthem at the Super Bowl, they require a microphone to be heard throughout the expansive stadium. Whenever a music producer mixes a new track, he or she uses electronic equipment. Electrical engineering is involved in nearly all parts of musical performance and production.

ACOUSTIC ENGINEERING

Some buildings are designed specifically for acoustic musical performances. Concert halls, recital halls, and opera houses are created with the same basic goal in mind: to make performers sound clear and authentic from every seat in the audience. They take into

CANCEL IT

Electrical engineers are responsible for some fascinating technology. One mind-blowing example is noise-canceling headphones. These amazing devices produced by companies such as Bose block out extra noise so sound quality is clear. They work by absorbing and analyzing the sound coming into the headphones and then creating a sound wave to block it out. Noise-canceling headphones can make it easier to hear your favorite tunes while you ride on a train or fly in a plane.

account the shape and size of the room, the materials of the seats, floor, walls, and ceiling, and acoustic objects such as sound shells. This allows sound waves from the musicians' instruments and voices to be naturally amplified by resonating. Resonating means to re-sound. As the sound bounces around the space, it picks up more and more sonic energy and sounds louder. The sound reverberates through the room until it is absorbed. The goal is to allow the sound to reverberate enough for it to reach all audience members without reverberating too much. If there is too much reverberation, it becomes an echo that makes the sound less clear. This phenomenon is evident in domed churches with marble floors and walls. After the initial sound stops, the sound continues echoing for a few seconds.

Creating just the right amount of reverberation isn't the only challenge facing acoustic engineers and architects who design these buildings. They must also be aware of the common phenomenon of acoustic hot spots and dry spots on the stage. This means that performers in one part of the stage might be heard perfectly, but performers in another spot might seem completely silent

Concert halls are designed specifically to make the sounds created on the stage clear and authentic for every listener in the audience.

to the audience. The best engineers design halls with uniform reverberation so that every instrument can be heard at all times.

In opera halls, engineers have the unique challenge of designing a space where each instrument in the orchestra can be heard clearly, without overpowering the singer. The most common way this is achieved is with an orchestra pit. Orchestra pits are typically just below the stage, a few feet below and in front of the audience. This allows the unamplified singers to be heard over the orchestra.

As if that weren't a difficult enough task, designers must also keep in mind the beauty of the hall. If the design is distracting or unattractive, it can pull attention away from the action on the stage. Performance spaces are created with beauty and practicality in mind.

Advancements in acoustical engineering have created some amazing innovations. Perhaps the most fascinating is the creation of something called "virtual acoustic environment" or VAE technology. VAE technology allows users to change the acoustics of a room with the push of a button. This technology is becoming more and more popular in university music departments. Students are able to practice their music in a space that sounds like an intimate recital hall, a grand cathedral, or an enormous concert hall, without leaving their practice room. This gives them the opportunity to learn how to use their instruments in a wide variety of spaces, which can be enormously beneficial.

Engineers of all different fields provide musicians with ways to make music come to life. Whether through the use of new instruments, sound amplification and manipulation, the creation of new software, apps, and games, new electrical capabilities, or acoustically designed performance spaces, engineers are a necessary component to the world of musical performance.

In a well-designed concert venue, audio technicians will have an easy night if the acoustical engineer did a good job when it was designed.

TEXT-DEPENDENT QUESTIONS

1. What does an Acoustic Engineer do?
2. Why are Sound Engineers important for live and/or recorded performances?
3. How is engineering involved in the creation of new instruments?

RESEARCH PROJECT

Observe and record the sound quality of music streaming through phone speakers. Move the phone to a small, round-shaped bowl. Next, place the phone in a cardboard box. Last, place the phone in an empty bathtub. Observe and record your results.

What impact did the container's shape and material have on the quality and amplification of the sound?

What are some other containers that could affect the sound quality and how?

WORDS TO UNDERSTAND

Monteverdi–Artusi Debate—the 17th century debate over which was most important between text and music

musical texture—how many instruments are playing and which ones

timbre—the tone quality of a sound

CHAPTER 4

ART IN MUSIC

Almost everyone on earth loves music! Seriously! It's so rare to dislike music that neurologists have even come up with a name for this strange disorder (amusia) and only a small percentage of the world's population has it. Music is one of seven disciplines that fit into a category called the arts. The Encyclopedia Britannica defines art as "modes of expression that use skill or imagination in the creation of aesthetic objects, environments, or experiences that can be shared with others." Basically, that's a fancy way of saying that art is imaginative, skillful stuff created by people to be shared with other people. There are so many different art forms that the arts are often divided into three categories: the literary arts, such as poetry and books, the performing arts, such as dance, theatre, and music, and the visual arts, such as painting, sculpting, filmmaking, and photography.

The arts are all intertwined. They all share the goal of communicating the way we think and feel about the world around us. They help us to tell stories. Each art form appeals to a different

The language art of songwriting is perhaps the most impactful art associated with music.

human sense: the language arts stimulate human intellect, dance makes use of the kinesthetic sense (the sense of how the body moves), the visual arts communicate via the sense of sight, and music delights the sense of hearing. Each of the arts has its own unique way of conveying human experiences. Since each art form has its own type of expression, multiple art forms often combine to make an even greater impact on the audience. So how do the various art forms contribute to how people experience music?

LANGUAGE ARTS

Of all the arts, the language arts might have the most noticeable impact on music. That's why it's so fun to memorize the lyrics of songs! The link between music and text goes back a long way. The **Monteverdi–Artusi Debate** is the debate over which is more important between music and lyrics. It began all the way back in the 1600s, when composer and music theorist Giovanni Artusi believed that music should take priority and poetry didn't matter. Famous composer Claudio Monteverdi, on the other hand, argued that words were more important. There was a whole big Twitter war (each "tweet" was actually a handwritten letter that took days to deliver).

The lyrics can be taken from a pre-existing poem, written to fit music that was already composed, or they can be written alongside the music. Sometimes lyrics are influenced by another artwork, such as a painting, play, or fable. For example, the Led Zeppelin song "Ramble On" is based on the fantasy novel *Lord of the Rings*. Other times, the text is written to describe something the composer has experienced. Some lyrics are romantic, some are patriotic, some are angry, some are heartbroken, and some are happy. Song lyrics can remind people of their fondest memories, or they can serve as a call to action. They can awaken a sense of spirituality or unite people with fellow fans of their favorite sports teams.

Song lyrics are not the only way the language arts and music are linked. Writers carefully choose specific words for advertisements, programs, or liner notes. Sometimes singers perform songs in foreign languages and they include translations on a screen or in a program. Sometimes video editors include subtitles on music videos. Enticing words flash across screens on advertisements for concerts or albums. Even band names, album names, and song names are important linguistic elements of music. A heavy metal band named Little Pink Bunnies would likely not get a lot of credit in the metal community. Word choice is *important.*

DANCE

The human connection to music is so innate that even babies respond when their moms drop a beat. So it makes sense that dance and music go hand-in-hand. Music can get toes tapping and hips wiggling. No wonder there's almost always music playing at parties! Many styles of music and dance go together quite naturally. Hip-hop dance expresses the emotional intensity of hip-hop music. Ballet originated to accompany the elegant music of 15th century Italy. Tap dance uses tap shoes as a percussive instrument to create music. Jazz music has its own smooth style of dance to go with it. Ballroom dance brings a whole new dimension to all kinds of different musical styles. Wouldn't it feel weird to slow dance to a fast song? That's because our bodies

Dancing is an innate human reaction to music.

Ethnomusicologist Kyra Gaunt discusses the culture surrounding the jump rope, including its cultural ties, its rhythm, and its lyrics.

instinctively feel rhythm. Only a small percent of the world lacks this innate sense, which neurologists call rhythm deafness.

Dance and music are inseparable. We see them together in movies and TV shows, in musicals, at sporting events, at concerts, at clubs, and at parties. If we're lucky, we might even catch a glimpse of an awesome flash mob every now and again. And as embarrassing as it may be to get caught rocking out in the car, sometimes, it's the only choice.

VISUAL ARTS

Music and the visual arts are linked in lots of ways. First, let's talk about how musicians use visual art: obviously, image is supremely important in the music industry. The way an artist dresses, applies makeup, and styles his or her hair is central to the image he or she is trying to create. It would be surprising to show up at a classical cello recital to find the cellist wearing a mohawk or a Lady Gaga costume. That's because musicians know that the way they look tells their audience something about who they are and what they will share through their music.

An artist's image is far from the only visual stimulation at a performance. Musical instruments can be ornate, colorful, or intricately carved. The lighting design of a concert adds drama and energy. Sometimes there are dramatic visual effects like pyrotechnics or bright screen displays. Even the way the performance venue is built can contribute to (or take away from) the

Pop star Lady Gaga has a unique style that is like a signature recognized by her fans.

ALBUM ART

The comeback of the vinyl record as a format for listening to recorded music also meant the comeback of the album cover concept. Once a key tool in marketing music albums, all but album art disappeared in the era of digital music delivered by electronic file or streamed via the Internet. Album covers have a long and colorful history. *Rolling Stone* magazine had readers rank the greatest album covers of all time. The top five choices were: 1) *Sgt. Pepper's Lonely Hearts Club Band* (1967) from The Beatles, 2) *Dark Side of the Moon* (1973) from Pink Floyd, 3) *Nevermind* (1991) from Nirvana, 4) *Abbey Road* (1969) from The Beatles, and 5) London Calling (1979) from The Clash.

visual aspect of the music. A stage may have colorful decorations, or holiday lights, or flowers bedazzling the audience. All of these things contribute to the visual aspect of music.

There are also plenty of ways that visual art ties into music before the performance even happens. There is swag such as posters and commercials, music videos and billboards, fliers, hats, shirts, bumper stickers, and key chains. Performers attach logos to their names. Their websites use high visual impact to attract fans.

Just imagine what movies would be like without music! Music provides important clues to give background information about the plot. Imagine how strange it would seem if, in the middle of an intense war scene, the "Hokey Pokey" began to play. Or if a victory scene were punctuated with Darth Vader's "Imperial March." It would feel confusing, perhaps even silly. If suspenseful music builds in the background while the protagonist of a movie is sitting lazily in a park, the audience can expect something unforeseen lurking in the shadows. Similarly, when the bad guy has been defeated at the end of a super hero movie, the music plays triumphantly and the audience knows the situation is safe. Music lends itself to film in a way that clarifies and deepens the emotions happening on-screen.

Visual arts also play a role in inspiring music. Composers often base their music on various forms of visual art. Some famous examples are Nat King Cole's "Mona Lisa," Don McClean's "Vincent," (based on the paintings of Vincent Van Gogh), and even Lady Gaga's "Venus," which pulls inspiration from a famous painting "The Birth of Venus" by Botticelli. Modest Mussorgsky composed his symphonic masterpiece "Pictures at an Exhibition" after he saw a collection of his friend's paintings. The visual arts and music go hand-in-hand.

Visual art like posters helps to create a mood for the listener before they even hear the music.

Music contains elements such as harmonies, melodies, rhythms, textures, tempos, timbres, expressive elements, and texts.

SOUND

It may seem redundant to include this category here (obviously sound is an important factor in creating music), but sound is involved in more ways than one might imagine. Music contains harmonies, melodies, rhythms, **textures**, tempos (speed of each piece), **timbres**, expressive elements, and texts. It is almost incredible that composers have created every piece in the universe using just these musical elements.

Melody and harmony are the foundation of songs. The melody is the superstar, the main character, and the one who tells the story. It's usually the part that the lead singer sings. The harmony serves as the supporting role. It's made up of all the notes that help the melody shine. Think of Imogen Heap's music or the song "Seven Bridges Road" by the Eagles. There are lots of notes happening around the central note. Those extra notes form a musical chord and that chord makes harmony. It doesn't stop there. Whenever there is more than one note playing, whether it's being sung or played on an instrument, those notes create harmony. So when a musician is on stage with just his or her guitar, that guitar is providing harmonies to spice up and support the melody. You can think of the harmony as a really important accessory. Sure, an outfit can be cute on its own, but until you add the perfect shoes and earrings, it just doesn't pop.

If you've ever heard an acoustic version of a song when you're expecting the electric one, you know the difference is pretty humongous. The texture and timbre of the music help to shape how it makes the listener feel. Take, for example, the difference between a Ray LaMontagne concert and a performance of a Beethoven Symphony. The thick texture of a Beethoven symphony communicates bold, intense emotions. The Ray LaMontagne concert

Two classical music symphonies can sound and feel vastly different due to differences in the texture and timbre of the music.

is likely to elicit subtler, more intimate feelings. On top of that, imagine the world of possibilities that opens up when you consider how a human voice affects the texture and timbre of music. Since voices come in all shapes, colors, and sizes, they can have a big impact on the overall sound of a song. Imagine replacing David Draiman with Frank Sinatra as the lead singer for *Disturbed*. It wouldn't sound quite the same, would it?

Music can be slow, fast, or in between. It can have a strong sense of beat or a gentle one. The beat can feel steady or sporadic and uneven. Rhythm is a big part of what dictates musical style. When someone in the next car over is listening to hip-hop, it's pretty unlikely that it'll be confused for Iron and Wine. The bumping, pulsing rhythm is a dead giveaway. Likewise, the commonly swung rhythms of jazz music make it easy to recognize and identify.

In most popular musical styles, amplification is a must. Pop stars often perform in huge auditoriums that were designed for sporting events. They are often expected to dance aerobically while they sing, so their vocal power is somewhat compromised. They're singing over thousands of screaming fans as well. If they didn't use microphones, they wouldn't be heard. Sometimes pop singers even lip-sync the music and play a recording through the loud speaker. There can also be sound effects included in the sound pumped through the speakers.

Classical musicians, on the other hand, typically perform unamplified. Opera singers train to turn their own bodies into an amplification system, so they can be heard in the back of a large hall, over an orchestra. Opera houses were built with this in mind. Architects design classical concert halls in such a way that the structure, itself, boosts the natural volume of the music. And because there's no external amplification system blaring out the music from the stage, the expectation is that the audience members should remain silent.

Music is a multifaceted art. It involves elements of all three branches of the arts: literary art, performance art, and visual art, with each of these elements contributing to music's awesome, communicative power. The literary arts provide lyrics, advertisements, and subtitles. The performance arts contribute dance, and of course, the music itself. The visual arts add stimulating graphic images, such as lighting, pictures, paintings, and pyrotechnics. Without these extra-musical disciplines, music wouldn't exist in the same way. So next time you see an exciting concert, look around and notice all the amazing details that allowed it to come to life. When it's over, make sure to thank *all* the artists involved.

Opera singers train so they can project their voices all the way to the back of the concert hall.

TEXT-DEPENDENT QUESTIONS

1. What are some of the different art forms that are commonly involved with music?
2. How do artists use visual arts in musical performances?
3. How do the language arts interact with music?

RESEARCH PROJECT

Choose a favorite poem or (even better) create a new one. Try to turn it into a song. Create a dance to compliment it. Record your observations.

Were there parts of this assignment that were difficult or easy? Did you use any unexpected skills?

Record the performance using a phone or other recording device. What did you notice? Did the recording match what you imagined? Record your answers.

WORDS TO UNDERSTAND

intervals—the time between two notes

measure—a unit of music with a prescribed number of beats shown in the time signature

note values—the duration (length) of a musical note

rhythm—the aspect of music comprising all the elements (such as accent, meter, and tempo) that relate to forward movement

CHAPTER 5

MATH IN MUSIC

Though math and music seem like they might be opposite disciplines, they are linked in many ways. Whether a musician is counting beats, playing or singing various **rhythms**, or giving information on sheet music, math is an important component of figuring out how sound works.

PYTHAGORAS

Pythagoras is remembered mostly for his contribution of the Pythagorean Theorem ($A^2 + B^2 + C^2$) but he, a 6th Century BCE Greek philosopher, mathematician, scientist, and musician, was uniquely able to make incredible observations about the connections between these two seemingly different fields. Pythagoras was the first person to notice (or at least to put in writing) that there is a relationship between the length of a string and its pitch when plucked. He observed that shorter strings vibrated at a higher frequency, therefore sounding at a higher pitch, and longer strings vibrated at lower frequencies, and therefore sounded lower. He looked closely at the ratio of a string and the frequency it produced, and his findings have helped us to understand how music works. Pythagoras' findings have shaped how instruments are made and how music is understood. For example, a violin's strings are shorter than a cello's. Therefore, it is pitched higher than a cello. When a guitarist presses down on a string, he or she is limiting which part of the string is vibrating. This is how string players change pitches on their instruments. Thanks to Pythagoras, musicians are able to tune their instruments so they sound their best.

Pythagoras also discovered the mathematical relationships between the **intervals** of the harmonic series of overtones. Overtones are frequencies that vibrate above the pitch that people hear and allow that sound to resonate or self-amplify. Different patterns of overtones also create different tone colors. More low overtones create a warmer, darker sound. More high overtones create a brighter sound with greater ring.

Ancient Greek mathematician Pythagoras was the first to make note of the relationship between string length and sound frequency.

MUSIC FUNDAMENTALS: NUMBERS IN MUSIC

The most fundamental component in music is the beat. It is the first thing beginners learn when they start to read music. They begin by counting a steady beat. 1,2,3,4 1,2,3,4 1,2,3,4. After they have begun to feel the steadiness of the beat, they learn that different types of notes have different **note values**, on lengths of duration. A quarter note lasts one beat. A half note lasts two. A whole note lasts four. An eighth note lasts half a beat. A **measure** is a rhythmic unit in a piece of music. Measures usually contain a fixed number of beats. For example, a song with 4 beats in every measure can be made up of measures with 4 quarter notes each, 2 half notes each, 8 eighth notes each, or 1 whole note each. As long as there are exactly the right number of beats in a measure, it doesn't matter which note values are used. Rhythm refers to how different note values are arranged in a piece of music. It can be made up of steady or sporadic beats. It can be simple and steady or incredibly complex. It can be fast, slow, or in between. Rhythm can make beats seem stronger or weaker. It can make a song feel crisp and percussive or soft and mellow.

When a musician reads a piece of sheet music, the pitch of the notes is determined by where they sit on a staff. A staff is a series of five stacked horizontal lines and the four spaces between them. It is then divided into measures. Each line and space on the staff represents a specific note. The musician's job is to interpret which note to play, for how long, at what volume, and in what style. Singers also incorporate text, sometimes in a foreign language.

In music, numbers are everywhere. At the very beginning of almost every piece of music, even before the first note, there is a time signature. Time signatures help musicians understand how to count

On sheet music, the pitch of the notes is determined by where they sit on a staff.

the music so that the rhythm is accurate. Time signatures are usually written like fractions, with one number directly above the other. They indicate how many beats exist in each measure and the note value of a single beat. For example, in 3/4 time, there are 3 quarter beats in each measure. Depending on the instruments, throughout the sheet music there may be instructions to use specific fingers to play a note so that the notes before or after it can be smooth and easy to reach. Sometimes music is written in parts or movements. These movements are usually numbered. People who play in orchestras are familiar with the terms "first chair" and "second chair." Choral singers know the difference between a first and second soprano, a first and second alto, a first and second tenor, and a first and second bass.

FREQUENCY

Each pitch vibrates at a different rate or frequency. The faster a pitch vibrates, the higher the pitch. The number of vibrations in a second

This video explores how Beethoven used math to compose music, despite his deafness.

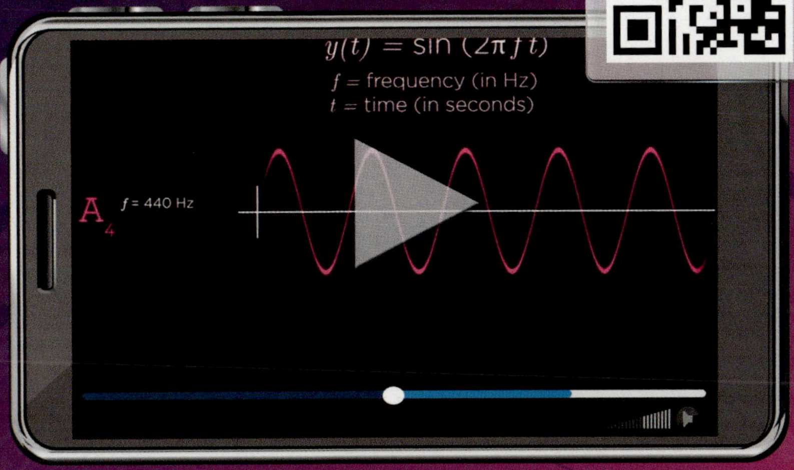

measures it. So the pitch A 440 vibrates 440 times per second. The A an octave above A 440 vibrates 880 times per second and so on. Today, musical instruments with fixed tuning (rather than adjustable tuning such as a guitar) are divided evenly between consecutive notes. Therefore, in a perfectly tuned piano, the goal is for each set of two neighboring notes to be the exact same distance apart. This system is called *Equal Temperament.*

SCALES AND KEY SIGNATURES

Most music is divided into scales. A musical scale is a series of pitches where the relationship between them is pre-determined. There are many different types of scales worldwide, but the ones most common to Western ears are major scales, which we usually hear in happy music, and minor scales, which we associate with sad

In a perfectly tuned piano, neighboring notes (or strings) will be the exact same distance apart.

music. The difference between these two scales is a small variation in two or three of the notes. Scales begin and end on the same pitch, an octave apart. For example, a C scale, whether major or minor, begins on C and ends on the next C. The pitches in between are what determine whether the scale is major or minor.

INTERVALS

The term interval refers to the space between two notes. Two neighboring notes in a scale are referred to as a *second*. The interval between two notes in a scale with a single note between them is called a *third*, etc. Unlike regular math, in music, a second plus a second equals a third and a third plus a third equals a fifth. Intervals can be consonant or dissonant. Consonant intervals sound relaxed together. Dissonant intervals sound tense. Composers use this information to create tension and release in their music. When intervals are played simultaneously, they form chords, which are important building blocks in music. Chords create harmonies. Whether or not we are aware of it, some harmonies sound stronger and some sound weaker to human ears. When writing a song, in order for the song to feel right to most listeners, a composer has to keep the strong and weak chords in balance. There are rules about how chords should progress. These rules are designed to guide composers to find the proper balance.

MUSICAL PATTERNS

Pattern recognition is an early building block of math education. In music, patterns are everywhere. Series of rhythms and notes often repeat throughout a piece of music. Pachelbel's famous piece *Canon in D* uses a repeating bass line (D-A-B-E-G-D-G-A) from start to finish. As this is happening, the music above the bass line evolves. The same bass line appears throughout modern pop music. Sometimes in theatre, specific rhythms or note sequences are associated with a specific character, place, or idea. For example, each time Darth Vader

Iconic foreboding music alerts viewers of the Star Wars movie saga to the impending arrival on screen of the villainous character, Darth Vader.

appears on the screen in a *Star Wars* movie, his theme plays in the background. Audience members begin to associate his character with his theme when they hear the music; so whenever the theme begins to play, they know that danger is looming. German composer, Richard Wagner, first used this phenomenon in operas. He called these themes "leitmotifs." Like in math, patterns in music help inform musicians and audience members about what is happening between the lines.

ACOUSTICS

The field of acoustics explores the way sound works. Acousticians, or people who study acoustics, are crucial to the music world. Their jobs vary from designing microphones and concert halls, to detecting and treating hearing impairment, to designing instruments with more desirable sound quality, and beyond. For many applications of acoustics, math is a central part of the job. For example, in order to create a perfect opera house, an acoustical engineer must be able to predict how long the sound will reverberate before it fades away. In designing instruments, an acoustician might modify the shape slightly to change the timbre, or tone color, of the instrument. They might choose to adjust the materials used to make the instrument. This can bring out certain tone colors and dampen others.

Before sheet music can become *music*, the musician must solve for all the unknowns. It's like solving an algebraic equation. Math is a foundational part of what allows music to exist. It provides structure and order so that music can be an effective form of communication. Math provides a frame so that music can grow artistically around it. Music is simply an artistic expression of math.

TEXT-DEPENDENT QUESTIONS

1. What contributions did Pythagoras make to the field of music?
2. What are overtones?
3. What is a musical interval?

RESEARCH PROJECT

Find a guitar, or any stringed instrument with frets will work. On the thickest string, which produces the lowest pitch, use your left hand to place one finger lightly over the string on the 12th fret. With your right hand, gently pluck the string. While conducting this experiment, try to find the answers to the following things.

1. What happens to the sound of the pitch?
2. What does this teach you about harmonics?
3. What is the result if you repeat this experiment at the 7th, 5th, and 4th frets?
4. Where else on the string can you find harmonics?

FURTHER READING

Anniss, Matt. *The Story of Pop Music*. Mankato: Smart Apple Media, 2013.

Coleman, Patrick. *The Art of Music*. New Haven: Yale University Press, 2015.

Franceschina, John. *Music Theory Through Musical Theatre: Putting it Together*. Oxford: Oxford University Press, 2015.

Powell, John. *How Music Works: The Science and Psychology of Beautiful Sounds from Beethoven to Beetles and Beyond*. Boston: Little, Brown, and Company, 2011.

INTERNET RESOURCES

http://www.exploratorium.edu/music/exhibits/index.html
A website that demonstrates the connection between science and music. It includes an interactive online drum circle, a mixer, and other hands-on musical scientific experiments.

https://mathsciencemusic.org/#/project/mathematics-of-music
An incredible website that links math, science, and music. It provides fascinating links and well-organized information.

https://you.dj
This website allows users to mix their own tracks.

https://datadragon.com/education/
This is a good resource for learning to read music and decipher musical instrument sounds.

https://nigelstanford.com/cymatics/behind_the_scenes.aspx
A resource for cymatics information and cymatic experiments.

EDUCATIONAL VIDEO LINKS

Chapter 1: http://x-qr.net/1KtZ

Chapter 2: http://x-qr.net/1LGJ

Chapter 3: http://x-qr.net/1L2Y

Chapter 4: http://x-qr.net/1JPM

Chapter 5: http://x-qr.net/1K9W

INDEX

AUTHOR BIOGRAPHY

Dr. Stefanie Anduri is a professional opera singer, university voice teacher, freelance writer, wife, and mom of two wonderful boys. She is passionate about exposing new audiences to music that they have never heard before and getting people excited about the vast communicative and connective power of music. Dr. Anduri's scholarly writings include her doctoral dissertation as well as other papers and articles on operatic performance practice. She also co-authors a blog with her husband titled *Opera Parents*. Dr. Anduri currently resides in Grand Junction, Colorado, with her family and teaches vocal music at Colorado Mesa University.

PHOTO CREDITS

Shutterstock.com

Pg. 1: Poznyakov, pg. 6: carlos castilla, 8: Otmar Smit, 9: AlexanderLipko, 10: Shawn Goldberg, 14: Krista Kennell, 15: Phovoir, 16: Don Pablo, 19: nmedia, 20, 66, 76, Ollyy, 22: DisobeyArt, 24: WSW1985, 25: Rad K, 26: Andrey Armyagov, 27: Igor Bulgarin, 30: mekcar, 31: Morphart Creation, 34: Sangoiri, 36: Rawpixel.com, 38: Mikhail Olykainen, 40: dimm3d, 42: Kristaps K, 44, 54: PrinceOfLove, 46: Gorodenkoff, 49: Martin Good, 50: Roman Rvachov, 52: Lopolo, 56: diignat, 58: Everett Collection, 60: ne2p1, 61: PopTika, 62: Stokkete, 64: Tracy Whiteside, 70: Wongsiri Subhayon, 72: PhotoHouse, 73: Stefano Buttafoco

Dreamstime.com

Pg. 12: Mel Surdin, 31: Aleksandr Korchagin, 45: Michele Ursi, 68: Mauro Rodrigues